Everyday Heroes

Police Officers

Nichol Bryan
ABDO Publishing Company

visit us at
www.abdopub.com

Published by ABDO Publishing Company, 4940 Viking Drive, Edina, Minnesota 55435.
Copyright © 2003 by Abdo Consulting Group, Inc. International copyrights reserved in all countries. No part of this book may be reproduced in any form without written permission from the publisher.

Printed in the United States.

Editors: Kate A. Conley, Kristy Langanki Cannon, Kristianne E. Vieregger
Photo Credits: AP/Wide World, Corbis, TimePix
Art Direction: Neil Klinepier

Special thanks to:

Joy M. Rikala
Director of Public Safety and Chief of Police
City of Minnetonka, Minnesota

Library of Congress Cataloging-in-Publication Data

Bryan, Nichol, 1958-
    Police officers / Nichol Bryan.
      p. cm. -- (Everyday heroes)
    Includes index.
    Summary: Describes the role, training, and duties of a police officer.
    ISBN 1-57765-860-4
    1. Police--Juvenile literature. [1. Police. 2. Occupations.] I. Title. II. Everyday heroes (Edina, Minn.)

HV7922 .B79 2002
363.2'2--dc21
                                                        2002025366

Contents

Who Are the Police?

Our world would be a very dangerous place if it weren't for police officers. Each day, they work to keep us safe. They prevent crimes, find people who break laws, and bring criminals to justice. Many times, police officers risk their lives to protect other people. They are true heroes.

Police officers do many types of jobs, but they all work to protect people. They are members of a police force. There are many different kinds of police forces. They exist in almost every country and community in the world.

Sometimes police officers have difficult tasks. They may have to chase people and put them in handcuffs. They may also have to arrest people and bring them to jail.

Police officers also work in their communities to build trusting relationships. They help us and keep us safe. They do their job because they care about others.

A deputy sheriff pets her K-9 partner between training exercises.

Early Police Forces

Some of the first police officers worked in the Roman Empire more than 2,000 years ago! In the Middle Ages, nobles hired **constables** to keep order on their land. The constables arrested people who broke the rules.

In 1829, the first modern police force was formed in London, England. These police officers went on foot patrol. They walked through the streets to prevent crimes and find criminals. They also helped citizens in trouble. The London police knew they needed the help of ordinary people. So they were kind and friendly to everybody.

Soon, other cities around the world started their own police forces. In the United States, the first police force was formed in New York City, New York, in 1845. As cities across the United States and Canada grew, they needed police forces, too.

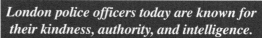

A London police officer helps a child cross the street.

London police officers today are known for their kindness, authority, and intelligence.

The first female police precinct in the United States was formed in New York in the early twentieth century.

Police Departments

Today, there are about 40,000 law enforcement **agencies** in the United States. Local police departments are based in towns and cities. They stop and prevent crime, keep order, and control traffic in their communities. They also work in schools as **liaisons**.

Sheriff's departments work in **counties**. **Deputy sheriffs** provide services for people who live outside of normal city **jurisdiction**. Deputy sheriffs control traffic on county roads. They also carry out court orders and help move prisoners from one jail to another.

State police officers have jurisdiction throughout an entire state. This means they can arrest criminals in any county or city. State police officers also patrol highways, stopping people who drive too fast or break other traffic laws. They help people who have car problems, too.

Local, county, and state police departments are funded by tax money. This means that police officers work for the people. Police forces at all levels must also answer to elected officials, such as mayors or governors.

Police departments must work with other government **agencies** to enforce laws. For example, they work with the courts. They often appear in court as witnesses. Police departments also work with federal, state, and local **prosecutors**.

In Minnetonka, Minnesota, Joy M. Rikala, Director of Public Safety and Chief of Police, is a key officer in her police department (below).

Police officers patrol the streets of New York City, New York (above).

Police Duties

Most police officers have many different duties every day. Many officers go on patrol. This means they walk or drive through an area alone or with a partner. Just by patrolling an area, police officers make it safer. Their presence warns criminals to stay away.

While on patrol, police officers must be ready for anything. They may need to stop a robbery or chase a fleeing suspect. They may help a stranded driver. They may also need to help at a traffic accident or give **first aid** to an injured person.

Officers in Los Angeles, California, map out a plan of action.

Watching traffic is another important part of a patrol officer's job. Some officers stay in one place and stop people who drive too fast. But any patrol officer may stop someone who is breaking a traffic law.

In addition to patrolling, police officers investigate crimes. They go to crime scenes and look for clues that will help them find the criminal. To get more clues, they talk to victims, witnesses, and suspects.

Police officers work to prevent crimes, too. They teach people how to be safe and how to prevent crimes such as burglaries. **Liaisons** visit classrooms to teach students about drug and violence resistance. Officers also work with neighborhood clubs that watch for crimes.

A police officer directs traffic during a blizzard in Tacoma, Washington.

Special Police Jobs

As police officers gain experience, they are responsible for more duties. There are several ranks of police officers. A police officer may go from patrol officer to sergeant, then lieutenant, and finally captain. Police officers in higher ranks manage officers in lower ranks. They may also have special jobs with specific duties.

Some officers become police investigators. Investigators solve crimes by gathering evidence and interviewing suspects and witnesses. They also conduct **surveillance** and even go **undercover**.

Police officers do other special jobs. Some work with young people to keep them out of trouble. They investigate crimes young people commit. Other officers may work to stop gang violence, catch drug dealers, or arrest drug users.

Some police officers investigate **white-collar crime**. Others have special skills for talking to criminals with **hostages**. Some officers are part of a bomb squad. Bomb squads are trained to take bombs apart and make them safe. Still other officers are trained to find missing people or rescue people.

A new police job is to patrol the Internet. Special officers catch people who use the Internet to steal money, hurt children, or commit other crimes.

An officer and his drug-sniffing dog search luggage at an airport.

A Police Officer's Skills

Police officers are very special people. They need to be physically strong to chase criminals on foot and restrain violent people. They also need to be honest and caring.

In addition, police officers must be good writers. They spend much time writing reports about what they do. These reports are often used as evidence in crime investigations and court cases. So officers must write their reports clearly and completely.

Police officers must also be observant. They need to notice small details that may be important clues. Police officers must also have keen memories. They have to recall many details accurately when they write reports or **testify** in court.

Police officers need to be good at communicating with all kinds of people. They need to be able to stay calm in stressful and dangerous situations. Often, officers can keep a situation from becoming violent just by talking the right way.

A patrol officer keeps order at a parade in Chicago, Illinois.

Education & Training

In the past, police officers needed only a high school education. Today, the job is much more complex. Many departments require people who want to be police officers to first attend college.

Police officer candidates must pass many tests. Some tests measure their health and physical strength. Other tests make sure candidates are mentally healthy and can tolerate stress. Background checks make sure candidates are honest people with no criminal history.

After passing these tests, new **recruits** usually attend a police academy. There, they study for months to learn how to prevent crimes, gather evidence, and handle a gun. They also train to be physically strong and to be skilled at jumping, climbing, and running.

Recruits attend a lecture.

Police officers need to be lifelong learners. They go back to school many times during their careers, and they learn more about their jobs while working. They learn about new police **techniques** and new laws that affect their jobs. They also learn about new technologies for investigating crimes.

An officer in Jacksonville, Florida, practices his gun skills.

Police Facilities

One important police facility is the police station. It is the center of police activity. The police station is a workplace for officers. It is also the place where police cars are kept.

The police station is where patrol officers get their assignments for the day. Investigators have offices there. The higher-ranked officers who manage the police force also work there.

A police dispatcher works at the police station, too. The dispatcher receives calls for help. Then the dispatcher sends patrol officers to the scene using a radio or computer.

Many other activities take place at the police station. Officers question suspects in interview rooms. Many stations also have holding cells. People under arrest stay there until they go to jail. And the police station is where officers write reports about the day's events.

Another important police facility is the crime laboratory. Forensic scientists work there. They use advanced equipment to study evidence. By looking at a bullet, they can tell if a suspect's gun was the one used in a shooting. Crime labs use fingerprints to identify people who were at a crime scene. Some crime labs can even test **DNA** to identify criminals.

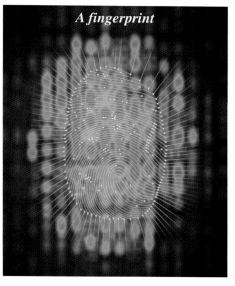

A fingerprint

A police sergeant closes the door to an empty jail cell.

19

Police Equipment

Police officers use many special kinds of equipment. One of the most important is their gun. Most police officers in the United States carry a handgun while on duty.

Police officers receive much training on using their gun. They are trained to shoot accurately. And they are trained

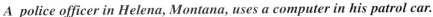

A police officer in Helena, Montana, uses a computer in his patrol car.

to know when to shoot and when not to. They may shoot a dangerous criminal if necessary in order to protect the public. This is called deadly force.

Police officers learn to use other weapons, too. They use rubber bullets, bean bags, pepper spray, and weapons that give criminals an electric shock. These weapons stop criminals without killing them.

Patrol cars have a lot of equipment officers use, too. They are designed for chasing suspects. They have flashing lights and sirens that warn people to pull over. Patrol cars also have radios, and some of them have computers. These allow officers to communicate with the station.

Patrol officers sometimes ride in **helicopters** when they need to patrol large areas. They ride bicycles or horses to patrol areas where cars can't go. Some police officers also travel with trained dogs called K-9 partners.

Police officers use advanced tools for investigations and arrests. For example, a **Breathalyzer** determines if a driver is drunk. And computer **databases** provide officers with information about criminals.

A Day's Work

Being a police officer is challenging. Police officers are needed 24 hours a day, seven days a week. That means that sometimes they work late at night, as well as during holidays and weekends. They need to work in all kinds of weather, too.

Sometimes police officers work in crowds, or even face **rioting** mobs. And they often have to deal with angry people. Sometimes, they have to deal with people who are suspicious of them.

Danger is often part of an officer's day. At times, police officers are injured

An officer and his K-9 partner patrol a subway in New York City, New York.

while trying to capture criminals. In high-speed chases, they risk crashing into cars or other obstacles. They must often use force to stop criminals. Sometimes, they even need to shoot criminals to protect innocent citizens, and themselves. Many police officers have been killed while doing their job.

While police work can be risky, it is also rewarding. Police officers say they like helping other people. They like keeping violent people off the streets and keeping drugs away from young people. They know their communities depend on them.

An Iowa state trooper on patrol

Making an Arrest

Police officers make an arrest when they believe someone has committed a serious crime. Sometimes, an arrest occurs when officers actually see someone commit a crime. Other times, an arrest occurs during an investigation when officers suspect someone of committing a crime.

When police officers make an arrest, they must follow special rules. They must tell the suspect why he or she is being arrested. They must also tell the suspect about his or her legal rights.

These rights include the right to remain silent. This means that the suspect doesn't have to talk to the officers about the crime. The suspect also has the right to have a lawyer present during police questioning. The officers must make sure the suspect understands his or her rights. Otherwise, the court case may be dismissed.

The arresting officers take the suspect to the police station. There, the suspect is photographed and fingerprinted. The suspect is then placed in a cell. Police officers might question him or her right away, or wait for a lawyer.

Then the officers write a report about the arrest. They may also attend a court **hearing**, when the suspect is charged with a crime. If the suspect goes to trial, the police officers may need to tell the jury about the investigation and arrest.

Fingerprints on a criminal record

A New York police officer and his K-9 partner walk a suspect out of a subway station.

The Police & You

Police officers work with the people in their communities. They talk to crime victims and witnesses. Officers talk to young people and run programs that help them stay out of trouble. They teach adults about driving safety and crime prevention. They even respond when burglar alarms sound in homes or offices.

People rely on the police to protect them. But the police also rely on the citizens. People can help the police in many ways. They can help by calling the police right away if they see a crime or suspicious activity. They can also help by answering an officer's questions if they witness a crime or accident.

In addition, citizens can help the police by volunteering to work in neighborhood watch clubs. People in neighborhood watch clubs stay alert in their communities. They call the police if they see anything unusual.

Neighborhood watch clubs help police respond to crimes faster. Also, criminals may avoid a neighborhood if they know it has a watch club.

Of course, people can help the police by obeying the law and driving carefully. People should also know that the police are there to protect and help them. People should always be courteous to police officers.

An officer in Bensalem, Pennsylvania, chats with a girl.

Safety Tips

Police officers often teach young people how to stay safe and avoid crime. Here is some advice many police departments give.

- Know your phone number and address, and the phone numbers of your parents at work.

- Ask your teacher or parent how to use 911 in an emergency.

- Don't talk to strangers and don't accept rides or gifts from them. A stranger is anyone you or your parents don't know and trust.

- If you spend time at home alone after school, call a parent or neighbor to check in as soon as you arrive.

- If you see anyone doing something that you think is wrong or that worries you, tell a parent, teacher, or another adult you trust.

 Remember that some adults use the Internet to hurt children. Don't talk to strangers on the Internet or give out your name, address, or phone number. To stay safe, make sure your parents always know what you're doing on the Internet.

 Don't let friends talk you into doing things you know you shouldn't, such as stealing, taking drugs, or damaging property. Remember that it's your life. Don't let anyone pressure you into making a dangerous mistake!

A police sergeant in Minot, North Dakota, helps kids collect evidence at a mock crime scene.

29

Glossary

agency - a department of the government.

Breathalyzer - a tool police officers use to determine how much alcohol is on someone's breath.

constable - a public officer responsible for keeping the peace.

county - the largest local government within a state.

database - a large collection of information.

deputy sheriff - an officer who works under the head sheriff.

DNA - a material in the body that is different for each person. Forensic scientists can identify DNA from a tiny sample of blood or hair found at a crime scene. This information can help show who was there, or who committed the crime.

first aid - emergency care given to a person before regular medical care is available.

hearing - the opportunity to present one's case in a court of law.

helicopter - an aircraft without wings that is lifted from the ground and kept in the air by horizontal propellers.

hostage - a person that a criminal holds against his or her will in order to make a deal with authorities.

jurisdiction - an area where a particular group has the power to govern or enforce laws.

liaison - a person who establishes understanding and cooperation between groups.

prosecutor - someone who charges suspects with crimes and presents cases to a judge or jury.

recruit - a newcomer to a field.

riot - a disturbance caused by a large group of people, sometimes with violence.

surveillance - a watch over someone's activities.

technique - a method or style in which something is done.

testify - to speak in a court of law while under oath.

undercover - acting in secret. Police officers do this sometimes by acting like criminals themselves to get inside information.

white-collar crime - crime committed by business people. It is often in the form of stealing money from their job.

Web Sites

Would you like to learn more about helping police officers keep your community safe? Please visit **www.abdopub.com** to find up-to-date Web site links that teach important safety tips. These links are routinely monitored and updated to provide the most current information available.

Index

DATE DUE

3/4/03 L.V.	
1-24-04 JS	